My Dream, America

Helen Munday

Copyright © 2017 Helen Munday

All rights reserved. No part(s) of this book may be reproduced, distributed or transmitted in any form, or by any means, or stored in a database or retrieval systems without prior expressed written permission of the author of this book.

ISBN: 978-1-5356-1007-0

I dedicate this book to my family and friends, who inspired me to write my story.

Table of Contents

Introduction vii

Chapter 1
South Africa 1

Chapter 2
The Journey 9

Chapter 3
New York, New York 13

Chapter 4
Canada 17

Chapter 5
Florida 29

Chapter 6
Texas 35

Introduction

It seems so long ago that I left the place called South Africa. "Sunny South Africa" once filled my spirit and soul with life. Growing up was a happy, loving, neighborly experience, but we were oblivious to the international indignation of South Africa's policy of apartheid. As a family, we feared the police interaction around us and, tragically, many hundreds of people died in the violence. Historical causes created antagonism between different groups. There were black radicals fighting with black moderates, as well as terrorist attacks by blacks on white South Africans and vice versa. It was and is a multinational population consisting of whites, blacks, Cape Colored's, Hottentots, Bushman, Indians from India, and Asians. Cape Colored's were defined under the apartheid regime. A minority group composed of persons of mixed race. The languages they speak are Afrikaans, Kaapse Afrikaans, and South African English. Ancestry includes European colonizers, indigenous Khoisan, Xhosa and slaves imported from the Dutch East Indies, Indonesia, Malaysia, Madagascar and Mozambique.

One important idea escaped us in South Africa: as Henry Ward Beecher said, "The real democratic American idea is, not that every man shall be on a level with every other man, but that every man shall have liberty to be what God made him, without hindrance." How could we understand or evaluate the circumstances and situations in which South Africa rallied, given that there was limited "media". There were two English newspapers and many written in Afrikaans, and a couple of radio stations, some were English, some were Afrikaans and no television.

South Africa, steeped in British tradition, influenced by the Dutch and the French both in education and religion, became a self-sufficient, successful country. Superstitions, different religions, and ancient folklore gave South Africa a colorful culture. It thrived due to extensive technology, mining (gold, diamonds, platinum, asbestos, chrome, uranium), and farming, both sheep (it has the fifth-largest wool clip in the world) and maize (corn; the first seeds were introduced from Amsterdam in 1655).

South Africa is located on the southern tip of Africa. The Indian Ocean in the east and the Atlantic Ocean in the west lap the coastline. Mountains surround the coastal belt on the edge of the interior plateau.

One can gaze and marvel at the beauty of nature, from towering, majestic mountains to forests, bays, waterfalls, rivers, lakes, and historical places. There is no place on earth with such a variety of rare plants, animals, and other wonders of nature as Africa. Most of this is concentrated at the Cape (the very southern tip of South Africa, where the Indian and Atlantic Oceans meet).

This was my home for twenty-one years. I was raised to speak English, Afrikaans, and Dutch, and I loved to learn and speak Zulu. My sister, who is five years older than me, was and is influential in my life.

My mother and her family were all born in Amsterdam, Holland. My mother's father, Opa, was a diamond cutter by trade and was contracted by De Beers to work with the South African diamond industry. My mother was nine upon her first arrival in South Africa, and two years after his contract expired, they all went back to Amsterdam, where Opa bought a small cigar shop. They lived upstairs. Just before WWII, my mother and the family came back to South Africa because they'd heard the rumblings about Hitler coming to the Netherlands. Opa cut diamonds for De Beers again. A few years later, he and two other diamond cutters formed their own diamond-cutting company, in Cape Town. My mother could not speak English but was determined to, and speak it well she did. She wrote with her left hand, but the teachers forced her to write with her right hand by tying her left hand behind her back to the chair. All left-handers went through the same struggle. Mom became ambidextrous. My sister and I are both left-handed;

thank goodness, teachers no longer tried to change us. My mother was determined that her children would speak and write English well; she said, "The world is English." We went to English schools, and it became our primary language. For that, I am eternally grateful.

We spoke some Dutch with my grandparents and Dutch friends. We had to learn to write, speak, and pass Afrikaans as a second language in all twelve grades of school. The Afrikaans schools had to do the same with the English language. All teachers had to be bilingual as well. Throughout South Africa, both languages were on all signs and notices in and out of the public areas.

My Dutch-speaking dad began his life in Indonesia. He and his twin brother were born in Buitenzorg, Java, West Indonesia. In 1814, the Kingdom of the Netherlands in Indonesia began. My great-grandfather was the Head of the Medical Services in Batavia, Java, Indonesia, and my grandfather was the Commissioner of Agriculture. There they lived and raised my father, his twin brother, his sister, and his older brother. On August 17, 1945, Indonesia declared its independence and the colonial rule of the Dutch East Indies ended. Japan then occupied Indonesia for a short time and the family moved back to Holland.

My dad's memoir, *The War Has Ended but the Memory Lingers On*, spans a five-year period during

World War II, and was co-authored and published by me. My dad came to Cape Town, South Africa, on his naval warship during World War II, where he met my mother. In 1948, he returned to Cape Town, and married my mother on July 3 of that same year. My Jewish mother and Dutch Reformed father remained married until 1955. The Dutch Reformed Church was the largest Christian denomination in the Netherlands from the time of the Protestant Reformation until 1930. The Dutch Reformed Church spread to the United States, Indonesia, Sri Lanka, Brazil, and South Africa. It was the original denomination of the Dutch Royal Family until merging into the Protestant Church in the Netherlands. The Dutch Reformed Church was a common feature among Dutch immigrant communities around the world, and became a crucial part of Afrikaaner Nationalism in South Africa.

    Sometimes my heart cries for the life of South Africa, the sounds, the earth, the smells, the beauty, and my friends. Africa touches and buries deep in one's heart and soul, and no one can take South Africa away from me. It remains etched in my heart, and here are some of my stories.

"Throughout the centuries there were men who took first steps down new roads armed with nothing but their own vision."

—Ayn Rand

Chapter 1
South Africa

The street lamp partially hid the white stuffed sock tied to a string. It was lying still on the hot asphalt. "Shhhh…" The sound of silence echoed as we huddled behind a large oak tree. My friends and I sat hunched and quiet, waiting.

"Here they come!"

As we slowly pulled the string, the white stuffed sock bobbed and glided across the street, shadowed by the dim streetlight. Screams of fear and running feet were heard, for what seemed to be a mile away in the opposite direction, as people ran back to where they came from. The game of "who thinks it's a snake" started again, and again, and again. Our tummies hurt from all the laughter. We played until our parents called us in to clean up and go to bed.

We loved to play outside in the street, and in the park, which had trampolines, a swimming pool, tennis courts, and a place to ride our bikes. The tennis courts had pressed red clay with whitewashed lines.

We played tennis with our wooden rackets and ate wild gooseberries growing around the courts, which made for great snacks. The one and only low water tap that protruded from the ground was used to water the clay courts, make tea, and quench our thirst. The little corner store was a long way away, so we had to rely on this tap. My mom would not let us wear blue jeans, drink "fizzy drinks" such as Coca-Cola, or eat out of a can. She was a gourmet cook, and we ate only fresh food, many fruits, and fresh fish from the fish market every Wednesday night. A rare treat was to get dressed up, go to the city, and eat at Wimpey's, where I ate a hamburger or grilled-cheese sandwich with a lime milkshake (my favorite).

We walked miles to school and back, our heavy, hard cardboard suitcases, filled with books, dragging hockey sticks, wooden tennis rackets, swim gear, and more. No school buses existed and there was no public bus route that would take us to school close to where we lived.

Jacaranda trees filled the streets and sky with a brilliant lavender-blue color in the summertime. Many "monkey weddings" happened in the summer (short, soft rain with the sun shining brightly). Summertime also brought on electrical storms that were fierce. The winter had many days of blue skies and sunshine.

It snowed once in my lifetime that I spent in South Africa. Everyone scrambled to build a tiny snowman. The higher altitude of Johannesburg, 5,751 feet, gave us a Californian climate. No central heat or air in any homes, and the winter cold was brutal to our fingers and toes. In the winter we would take a small hot bath at night (which we shared, Mom first, then my sister, and then me, as the severe droughts made water scarce--it would sometimes not rain for two to three years, and we would watch the clouds roll in and roll out with not a drop of water hitting the ground). In the morning, we would take turns plugging in the asbestos heater and throwing our clothes over it to warm them, then get up and hurriedly get dressed.

When I turned fourteen, we had to move from our duplex of fourteen years, as it had sold. We had nowhere to go. There was an old house down the road with an overgrown old shed, and the woman living in the house offered the shed to us at a small rental fee, which my mom could afford. It had no running water or indoor toilet. My sister and I prayed and prayed that we would not have to live in that old shed. Then someone offered to help Mom, and we moved to a tiny two-bedroom apartment in a suburb far away from Bez Valley. It took two public buses to get to my all-girls high school. I did not want to go to a school nearer to where we lived, as it was a mixed boy's and girl's high school, and I was very shy. In the cold winter, in the rain, in the heat, I stood waiting for public buses to bring me to and from school, leaving home at six in the morning and getting home between seven and eight o'clock in the evening, after piano lessons, hockey, swimming, tennis, and netball (a game similar to basketball).

Every Christmas, in the summertime, my mom, my sister, and I rode the train a thousand miles from Johannesburg to Cape Town and back, to our grandparents, cousins, and friends. My sister was born in Cape Town and I was born in Johannesburg. We lived in Johannesburg, but our grandparents, family, and friends lived in Cape Town. Every year Mrs. Curry would teach my sister and me to swim in a tidal pool in the ocean, at Kalk Bay. When we visited and swam in Fishhoek Beach the water was warm from the Indian Ocean, with streaks of icy water as the Atlantic and Indian Ocean joined there at Cape Point (very close to Fishhoek).

I loved the clickety-clack of the train, the wind blowing on our faces in our sleeper car, the narrow passageway and the food in the dining car. I enjoyed looking at the railway tracks speeding under us through the toilet hole when I stepped on the steel pedal to flush. I spent hours looking out of the windows at the different terrain. At night, we closed the windows; otherwise, the soot from the locomotive would cover us by morning. It covered us anyway. I would lie and listen to the sound of the steel wheels on the tracks and feel the sway, which rocked me to sleep. It took two or three days to get to our destination, depending on whether it was the milk train, which would stop at every small and nonexistent town to deliver milk in the Karoo Desert. Looking out the window in the Karoo, I would see the terrain had small cacti, shrubs, many rocks, sand, and maybe one small house in view. Near the end of the train journey, the train winds through tunnels, through the mountains and then all of a sudden, out of the dessert, the terrain changes and a most beautiful sight of vine yards and wild flowers appear, a part called the Garden Route of the Cape. This journey was the highlight of every year.

    Back in Johannesburg after the Christmas summer holidays, a new year of school would begin. Excited to see all of our friends and exchange holiday stories.

Helen Munday

One day I had a terrible pain in my stomach. My mother gave me the usual treatment for stomach aches, a saucer filled with burnt brandy. Dr. Ribinowitz made a house call and said I had to go to the hospital and have surgery.

My eyes were heavy and I was groggy from the anesthesia. I'd had my appendix out. I thought I was seeing things. My dad was sitting beside my bed, a rare visit. It was rare to get a visit from my Dad, as he worked in Persia for many years for British Petroleum, and some years he worked in South Africa.

"Hi," he said.

"Hi, Dad, I had a wonderful dream. I dreamt I went to America."

"America?" he answered, surprised. "Why do you want to go there? It is a mess. I think the pain medicine is making you have dreams, because at thirteen years old, how are you going to America?" It was 1968, and the United States was going through many changes. In my mind, I determined that I would one day visit America.

I felt very groggy, but my dad and I continued to talk a little about the crazy dream I had. The dream of coming to America never left me. I had no idea how vast it was in the United States.

My Dream, America

My dad's twin brother had migrated with his family and settled in the San Rafael, California, area. My cousin, who was my age, started writing to me and we sent each other tapes with our voices and interesting things about how we lived. I loved it. It was not often, but I would get so excited to hear about America.

I started making jewelry pendants out of baked clay, with leather thongs for the necklace, in all colors and designs and then selling them to get money to go to America. My mom would take them to work and sell them for me. The people in our neighborhood bought them as well. At the end of that year, I had made a little over the equivalent of a hundred American dollars (a hundred rand). I was never going to make enough money to go to America!

Years went by; I completed high school at age sixteen, and then went to nursing school to become a registered nurse and midwife, or a "sister," as they called us, which means a nun in the United States. When I first came to the United States, I would tell people I was a sister, and they would say, "That's nice." I found out later people had no idea I was saying I was a registered nurse; they thought I was saying I was a nun. At that time, nurses were the lowest paid profession in South Africa; next was teachers.

I kept dreaming of America.

Chapter 2
The Journey

Working double shifts back to back at the hospital, teaching children to play the guitar, playing squash and coaching squash, I scrambled to gather money to go to America. Finally, I saved sixteen hundred dollars, applied for a visa, and booked a flight that left June 1, 1977.

Family, friends, and a boyfriend came to say goodbye to me at the Johannesburg Airport. I weighed my suitcase and it was fifty dollars over in weight. I did not have the money for this extra expense, so I looked around and my boyfriend paid it. I assumed it was a goodbye-and-good-luck gesture.

My guitar was snuggled in a small closet in the front of the plane, my suitcase was in the belly of the plane, and I was squashed in the middle of a jumbo jet. I held on to my plane ticket as we ascended from the Johannesburg airport. Five years would pass before I would again see my family and the city where I was born. With my ticket for one year to America, a visa for three months, and sixteen hundred dollars, I was off on one of the grandest adventures in my life. I was finally off to America.

Our first landing was Nairobi, Kenya, a collection point for passengers. Everyone got off the plane, as it needed fumigation (for mosquito's and tsetse flies that carry diseases). This was 1977 and the rest of the world did not like white South Africans, due to all the political unrest, apartheid, and riots. South Africans were sheltered from the atrocities that occurred, as the news media was small and controlled. We did not see or hear much and there was limited freedom of speech. South Africa did not have television until 1975, and then it was only for an hour at night for the first year. Not many people could afford a television.

In the Nairobi airport, we South Africans stood in a circle, AK-47s pointed at our backs. Nairobi Airport appeared run-down and dark. I reached into my handbag for a cigarette, and suddenly I heard *click click* and was looking straight down at an AK-47 pointed at my belly, and also feeling one in my back. I froze with my hand still in my handbag. An unspoken bond forms between people during frightening situations. Finally, we all boarded the plane. There was a silence of fear and relief as the plane ascended.

My Dream, America

The plane landed in Luxembourg the following morning and I had an eight-hour layover. I washed my face, brushed my teeth, and fell asleep in the airport on a couple of chairs with my huge suitcase beside me and one hand clutching my guitar.

Iceland was my next destination. I spent a day in this astonishingly beautiful, green land. I promised myself that one day I would return to visit, but never have.

We flew over Greenland. I pressed my face against the oval window of the plane, staring at the white with variations of icy blues stretched from coast to land. I remember wondering why Iceland was green and Greenland was icy.

I must have fallen asleep, only to hear, "Fasten your seat belts and prepare for landing." As I again pressed my face against the window, the Statue of Liberty came into view. *Wow!* I thought. *I do hope I get to see her!* I had no preconceived ideas about any place in America; I just thought that everyone had a huge car, a fancy house, and a lovely life. I did not know how vast the United States was, nor how diverse the cultures.

Chapter 3
New York, New York

I was excited to be standing on the ground of the United States of America, tired and scared as I entered the New York airport. It had been fifty-two hours since my takeoff in Johannesburg; my heart was pounding.

"Open up your suitcase," I heard a stern voice say.

All I owned came tumbling out. I was fighting back my tears, thinking, *how am I going to get everything back into my suitcase?* It had taken three adults to sit on it and close the bulging hunk of leather just moments before the plane took off in Johannesburg.

"Everything's OK, you may pack up and go," said the immigration officer.

Go? I thought. *Thank you very much, all my belongings have fallen everywhere.*

"Lady, pack it up," said the officer. "Move along."

Move along? How heartless! Well, I thought, *I should be used to heartless*, because South Africa, as a police state, was stringent.

I rolled my clothes into little rolls back into my suitcase, and squashed, sat, squashed, and sat on my suitcase until it closed. I then proceeded out of Immigration and out into the public area of the airport.

"Helen, its Eva, Eva, your aunt."

It was my mother's cousin, a small, dark-haired, attractive woman. My uncle and aunt lived and owned an art shop in Manhattan. My uncle was an artist and interior designer. Eva and I snuggled into a taxi heading through New York.

"Aunt Eva, I thought everyone in America owned a car, a huge car."

She reached over and gave me a loving hug (which I needed), and reassured me that not everything was like the American movies my imagination was relying on.

That night I met my cousin and we watched television in color. Back home in South Africa color TV had just started running, for only one hour at night. I was awed by it, especially since the first time I'd seen a television show, *Monty Python*, it had been in black and white, and I was not impressed and had wondered why anyone would want to watch a jumping screen when there was so much to see and do. I'd seen it in London, when a friend and I, at age seventeen, had taken a hitchhiking trip through Europe, fourteen countries in all. What an adventurous trip! I was unafraid of the world.

"Let's see New York tomorrow," suggested Aunt Eva.

My family was so kind as to take me all over New York City, on a Hudson River tour, to the Statue of Liberty, to Manhattan and Central Park.

That evening I entertained my aunt and uncle with the many folk songs I had written in South Africa. I had thought producing them in the United States would be exciting. But, shy, ill prepared, with no experience in the competitive music industry, I stopped trying and just enjoyed the city and my newfound family.

Every day we shopped for dinner at a store in the street level of the apartment building. The carrots and other vegetables looked so clean compared to the vegetables in South Africa, which always had dirt on them.

Johannesburg is a bustling city, the engine of business in South Africa, but nowhere near as overwhelming as New York. I started to feel suffocated by the bustle and confusion of this pulsating, insomniac city. I did not feel peaceful in New York; it was time to move on.

Chapter 4
Canada

It was good-bye, New York and hello, Vancouver, Canada. The air was crisp yet warm as I stepped out of the plane in Vancouver. I was to meet my friend and her family, who had moved from Johannesburg to a small town called Tsawwassen. We had been in nursing school together.

This place called Tsawwassen, meaning "facing the ocean", although I was told it meant "land of sunshine" was beautiful, snuggled in logging country and surrounded by the Canadian Rocky Mountains. The air was crisp, clean, and drifted through my body in slow motion. The streets were clean and the people warm and friendly. This was where I would stay for many weeks. My friend and I were going to travel together, but to my surprise, I learned that she was pregnant and getting married. Sadly, soon after I arrived, she left Canada. Here I was all by myself, miles from home. Her family was kind and as hospitable as they possibly could be.

"It's hard to be an American," my friend's mom told me. "What do you plan to do?"

"What *do* I plan to do?" I sighed, filled with disheartenment.

I went upstairs to think about this while I sat with my feet dangling from my bedroom window ledge. It was midsummer, and I stared at the dark sky filled with Northern Hemisphere stars. This sky was new to me and I did not recognize any constellations; they were plain old stars to me. Maybe I would learn all about them one day.

"I will play it by ear, and sleep on what is to come next."

There were many wonderful things to do and see in Vancouver. I bought a set of oil and acrylic paints and some boards to paint on and began painting. I climbed the mountains, and walked around the beautiful city. Then I bought a secondhand car, a 1967 white four-door Datsun, for five hundred dollars. This helped me be independent and venture around Vancouver and Tsawwassen.

When I woke up one day, I decided to take a camping trip through the Canadian Rockies. The tour bus had blue tents that rolled out from the roof of the bus on either side. This was my first real Canadian adventure. Nearly every person that sat in

My Dream, America

the bus was from a different country; we spoke all different languages. It reminded me of Noah's Ark, except sometimes there was only one of each creature. The bus driver's name was "Billy Boy." I was from South Africa; one person was from Ireland, two from Germany, two from the States, two from Canada, and one from Finland. The first stop was the Kamloops.

At night, we would stop and roll out the tents off the roof of the bus. Our cots would be against the sides of the bus, women on one side, men the other. It looked like a flying elephant when set up. The beauty of the Rockies, the friendship of the group, and just the wonderful adventure erased all my anxieties. As we drove through the Rockies, past the crystal-blue rivers and lakes, I decided right then that I was coming back to all of this. I felt so free and unafraid; the presence of God was right beside me. I knew then that Jesus Christ, my Lord and Savior, would be with me and protect me from harm. I never felt afraid again. There were times when I felt lonely, though not alone, as many people surrounded me. I longed to share this with someone I knew. We traveled through the provinces of Columbia and Alberta to Calgary. All along the way, we encountered bears, moose, deer, mountain goats, and raccoons. I had never seen a moose or a raccoon before. There were times I was so cold, I had to buy warm woolen socks and a warm outfit. It was summer, but the glaciers were cold and it snowed one evening near Banff. The coldest area was the Columbia Icefields Parkway, filled with glaciers.

"What is that?" I whispered to someone on the next cot one night.

"I don't know," she whispered back.

We both whispered together, "*A bear!*"

"Quiet, they want food. The food is in the trees," said a very soft male voice from under the bus, on the other side.

What was that I said about being unafraid? My heart seemed to stop and so did my breathing. All that was between us and the bear was a blue piece of canvas. Oh, my goodness, the bear was sniffing near my feet. I froze. It seemed like *forever* until the bear left my feet, then our camping bus.

"It was a brown bear, not a grizzly. We would not have had a chance if it were a grizzly bear," said our bus driver/cook while making pancakes. "Usually the grizzlies don't come down this far, but one never knows."

Pancakes covered in syrup were new to me for breakfast. A sweet breakfast was different for me, as I was used to savory food in the morning. This was the dangerous beginning of my love for pancakes. A pancake in South Africa was a crepe, and a small, thicker, round pancake known as a flapjack, they were a rare treat.

We traveled to Calgary, Alberta, and back to Vancouver. Our journey continued and we all formed close friendships with each other. I kept up with three travelers after the fourteen-day adventure.

To the west of Tsawwassen is Point Roberts, which is in the United States, so one needs a passport to go there. It was just a few miles from where I lived and I loved going there. The beach was beautiful and I would take long walks, breathing in the fresh, crisp air. I felt so peaceful; the Gulf Islands came between the mainland, which made it calm. I watched the snow-capped mountain of Mount Baker in Washington from that beach many times. It looked just like an ice-cream cone. Here it was summer and I was looking at snow on a mountain. The low tide would retreat and one could walk a long way out.

Then one day I decided that the Gulf Islands needed exploring. The calm Gulf Island Sea connected to each forest-filled island, Vancouver and Victoria Island. After arriving on the ferry at Galiano Island, I drove my car onto the small road. The colors and beauty that surrounded me were magic. The days to follow were days of a lifetime.

I found an overgrown gravesite and a small church. I cleaned up the gravesite for ten dollars, and this paid for gas and food. I slept in my car off the road, and the next morning while driving slowly around the island, I stopped and looked at the houses and trees. I gazed across the ocean to another island and wondered what was on the other side.

It was a cloudy, warm morning. I was walking along a small-pebbled shoreline, and looked down. *What was that?* I heard a noise I had never heard before. As I walked, I discovered that it was a baby seal, or I thought it was a baby seal. I bent down and looked at it, and wondered why it was just lying there, with no mother or other seal friends. Not knowing anything about seals, I tried to pick it up.

"Goodness, you're heavy." I guessed about sixty to seventy-five pounds. Finally, with all my strength, I scooped her up and named her Sammy. It sounded sweet. I placed her in the back seat of my car, and drove to the nearest house.

"Boy, you stink, Sammy."

She grunted, or barked or whatever the sound was. She made noises. I stopped at the nearest house and knocked on the door, not realizing that I myself now stank of Sammy.

My Dream, America

"Excuse me, I need help. Sorry to bother you, but do you know anything about seals?" I asked.

"When a mother seal has twins they sometimes dump one if she cannot take care of two. Here is a metal washtub. You need to fill it with water, to keep her eyes wet, but try and release the seal as soon as possible. It is not legal to just own a seal."

"I don't want to own her, just help her."

So from island to island, for approximately three weeks, Sammy and I traveled and slept in the car. I would take her to the ocean many times a day and she would swim around, but not swim away. I fed her sardines, which most times she did not want; I would fill a baby bottle (with a tiny teat) with human-baby powdered milk. When I saw someone fishing, I would feed her live bait. We had great conversations together. I would sing and she would bark. I imagined Sammy was singing along. No one bothered me, as my car was very smelly. One day I took Sammy to swim and she swam around, and then I watched as she disappeared into the ocean. I waited there until morning. She just simply swam away. At the very moment when the sun came up, I cried, happy and sad tears.

After many weeks of moving about the islands, I headed back to the mainland, Vancouver. I decided to travel back through the Rocky Mountains on my own. On the camping trip I'd met a few people, and decided to re-connect with them in Calgary.

I painted with acrylics (on anything I found), and wrote songs as I travelled. I learned about the game football. Canadian football and American football had some differences. The celebration of the football game was fascinating to me. The excitement and enthusiasm was at first a little overwhelming––the bands, the cheerleaders, and the excitement of the crowd. I did not grow up around soccer or rugby, as I had no male figures in my life.

My Datsun tended to have mechanical difficulties at times. The fan belt broke a few times and I used pantyhose to replace the belt. The radiator once developed a hole in it and I used a bar of soap to plug the hole. Overall, it served me well.

It was raining and my car had stopped running. I was near a small shopping strip mall, near Calgary. I ran to a phone booth and shut the door. I stood and watched the rain come down. Sliding to my haunches in the booth, I cried. I had no one to call, not much money, and I was hungry. I remember crying softly and saying, "Oh God, help me." I had no idea how much time went by. It did not matter. Finally, I composed myself, stood up, and walked out of the phone booth to a store nearby.

"Please, I need some help," I said to the store clerk.

I told her my story. I must have looked pitiful. She said she had a friend that fixed cars. I told her I could pay with a case of Blues Beer (a Canadian beer) someone had given me that was in my boot (trunk). The store clerk's friend came to where my car was and they towed it. They accepted the case of Blues Beer, and offered a place to sleep for the night.

"Thank you, Lord," I said once again.

They were so kind. I stayed a few days upon their request and I was forever grateful. I reckoned then with myself that I could never return the favor to the people who'd helped me in life so I would just help anyone I could with no obligation to return those good deeds, and to this day, I have done that.

I was on my way to the Okanagan Valley, where I picked fruit for some extra money. It was hard work. I continued my journey in a few weeks and stopped many times, watched, and swam in the cold, blue, beautiful lakes and rivers. Watching fly fishermen, I realized how skillful and precise this sport seemed to be.

I left the valley, and while winding through the mountains I saw someone sitting on the side of the road. I stopped. She was a vagabond and her name was Kathleen. She was from Ireland and her husband, who used to travel with her, had recently died. She was much older than I was, and she wrote books (in rough copy) and sold them. She was an English professor from Ireland. She came to Canada and just traveled. Kathleen climbed in the car and off we went. We traveled together for three days. We shared meals together and slept in the car. It was good to have company in the car with me. I slept in my car most of the time and cleaned up at the truck stops.

"I want you to meet some friends of mine. They live in Kelowna, beautiful farming country," she said. Then we drove to a farm surrounded by huge trees. It was so beautiful it could have been a painting. I was shy and not used to this, but I followed Kathleen into this beautiful farmhouse and met a most endearing family.

We had beds to sleep in, a hot bath (what luxury), and delicious supper and breakfast. Home-cooked meals--I felt like a princess.

The next day, Kathleen and I said goodbye at the Kamloops. Not far out of the Kamloops, on my way to Vancouver, I gave a ride to two boys, who had just finished high school and were on an adventure to Vancouver. This was good company all the way back to Vancouver. We played the guitar and swapped stories and dreams of our future.

My Dream, America

I'd made this trip through the Canadian Rockies to Calgary three times. I had seen Lake Louise three times, and the train winding through the mountains. I love trains. *I am coming back to Canada someday to travel the Canadian railway from east to west*, I told myself.

I decided to go to Florida, as my stepbrother, who lived there, told me it was a possibility I could get a working visa there at the Gainesville Hospital, as a nurse. I had run out of money and needed to sell my car but did not know how. I sat in a Denny's restaurant in Vancouver with enough money for a small meal and coffee. Never-ending coffee, this was great. I decided to make a paper sign with the details of my car on some paper the server gave to me. I laid it on my table.

It read, "$400.00 1967 Datsun for sale. In three months, I put 3,400 miles on the car. Need money to fly to Florida, as soon as possible." Hours went by; people stopped and chatted, but no luck. Close to 6:00 a.m., a man sat next to me and asked about the car. Almost twenty-four hours had gone by, and I made the sale, cash. We went to the title company and made the exchange.

I bought an airline ticket to Gainesville, Florida, and had $60.00 left in my pocket. After a good meal, I cleaned up and headed for the Vancouver airport.

Chapter 5
Florida

It was a long journey back into the United States. I wanted to see everything despite my lack of finances and I would give it my best shot.

As I sat in mid-air flying to Florida, I felt as if I had a fever. There was a terrible pain in my back and the person next to me was concerned that I might need to see a doctor when I landed. I felt embarrassed and alone as I got sicker, so when my stepbrother and his wife greeted me I tried not to show that I was ill. Both were doctors in biochemistry. They were working on research at the hospital in Gainesville for a one-year contract, and then they were moving to London.

A few days passed and I was so ill that my family took me to the hospital. The doctor wanted to admit me, as I had a severe case of pyelonephritis (kidney infection), but it was a private hospital, and I had no insurance or money. They gave me a prescription for some antibiotics and painkillers, and then an antibiotic intravenously. I was so grateful for my family, who helped to pay for everything and took me home. Because my family worked every day, I had to walk to and from the clinic to receive intravenous antibiotics. This continued for a week and after each walk home, I curled up on the cushions on the floor that was my bed. Once again, I was embarrassed, as I could not repay them. I owed my life to my family but despite them, I felt lost and lonely. I tried to get a work permit so that I could get a job in the hospital, but this was 1977 and Florida did not even have enough work for the Floridians. I raked leaves and babysat for some money.

Shortly after that, I met a friend, Trevor, who invited me to travel to Naples, Florida, to see some of his friends.

While we were there, Trevor said, "There are some great sandbars out there, and you could snorkel while I scuba dive and find all kinds of sea urchins."

We left the Naples shoreline in a small rowboat that belonged to my new friends. We rowed our way through the canals, which had houses and cypress groves on either side. It was a beautiful hot day. Finally, we got to a sandbar in the ocean, and snorkeled and swam for hours, losing all track of time, tide, and weather. It was near the end of the day.

"Trevor, one of the oars has drifted away!" I shouted.

My Dream, America

"Get the boat and the other oar!" he shouted back.

"The other oar has gone as well," I fearfully called back.

"Pull the boat toward me, take the rope and swim, it is the only way!" Trevor shouted as he swam toward me. "The tide is in and we are screwed."

My heart pounded as I looked up at the sunset. I was fit and a good swimmer, but this seemed beyond my strength. I put the rope that tied to the boat around my waist, and started swimming toward Trevor, who was closer to the shoreline. When I reached him, he told me to climb into the boat and he placed the rope around his waist and swam, pulling the boat with me in it. We were now close to the mouth of the canal and Trevor, exhausted, came back into the boat, and I tied the rope around my waist and swam. We took turns until we could reach the ocean floor; we walked, swam and pulled. Finally, we entered the mouth of the canal, guided by the dim light from the sunset; the cypress groves were on either side of us. I did not have water shoes on as Trevor did and I could feel things that scraped against my feet and legs at times; I dared not think about what they were. Dehydrated, sunburned, thirsty, hungry, and just plain exhausted, Trevor said, "We still have a long way to go. Just don't think and pull."

He had to take over when we were a little deeper in the canal, as it split in three. I would not have known which part of the canal to go through. It was now pitch dark. We were not near the houses yet.

"Trevor, there's a light. It sounds like a boat. Do we have a flare or anything like that to attract them?"

"No," he shouted back to me.

We started yelling, "Hello, help!" I just did not have the strength to shout very loudly.

"Trevor, you get in the boat and shout while I pull and swim with the boat."

He climbed into the boat and I climbed out again. I was just getting the rope around my waist when Trevor shouted, "Help!"

"Hello there, this is the Coast Guard, are you OK?" We were so exhausted when the Coast Guard came up to our boat. Thank you, Lord!

The Coast Guard wrapped us in blankets, gave us water, tied our boat to theirs, and headed to the house. The Coast Guard wanted to hospitalize us, but I was afraid to go, as I had no money and no medical insurance. Medical care was sent to the house, as Trevor's friend was a doctor. We were treated and inside for days. Sunburn, dehydration, heat stroke, and nausea made it impossible to know how many days went by. After recovering, we drove back to

My Dream, America

Gainesville and again I felt helpless regarding work in the States.

I still had very little money, only the few dollars from racking leaves and babysitting. How would I be able to get my visa renewed, live, and travel if I did not work? If I went back to South Africa, I would never get enough money together to come back to the States. Texas, yes, what about Texas!

The only advertisement (in a South African medical magazine), regarding working in America was for a Texas nursing agency in Houston. I had sent all my nursing papers to the agency while I was still in South Africa, so I called them, asking them if they still had my nursing-college papers. I would work anywhere and any shift. They had my papers, and within a few weeks, I was flying to Big Spring, Texas, to work the night shift. I had a working visa as long as I attended college to get my Texas RN license.

Chapter 6
Texas

I had no earthly idea where I was going, as I knew nothing about Texas. Midland-Odessa airport was small. Everyone climbed down the stairs of the plane and walked onto the tarmac to the entrance of the airport. My heart was beating so fast. I'd told the agency that I was tall with red hair and would be wearing a black pinstriped jumpsuit. The airport cleared at dusk and I stood alone in the airport, waiting with my suitcase and guitar. Finally, I approached a couple standing and looking around and asked if they were waiting for me.

"Yes, we are," they said, "but you are not black and not wearing a red jumpsuit; since you're from Africa, we assumed you would be black."

I responded, "I told the agency that I would be wearing a black pinstriped jumpsuit and was tall with red hair," and we all laughed.

We drove for many miles; the darkness and rumble of the car made me sleepy. There were very few lights from houses off the road. Finally, we approached what looked like a bright, enormous city. This was Big Spring, and that was not a city but a huge oil refinery. I had never seen this before. South Africa did not find oil until early 1997, and on August 7, 2003, Sable Mining Africa changed all that. The company Sasol, founded in 1950, made coal-to-petroleum that helped supply some of South Africa's oil needs.

The Air Force base had closed a few years before in Big Spring, and the old, small barracks helped supply housing for the local Big Spring population. They brought me to one of these barracks. "We hope this will be all right for you; we will deduct the rent for this month from your first paycheck."

"Yes, thank you so very much," I said wearily.

"We will see you on Monday at that hospital on the hill."

They left. I had no money and no idea what this new adventure would bring. With the key in my hand, I stood and looked at this little place. It had a small living room with a couch, a tiny kitchen with a table, a bedroom with a bed, a bathroom with a closet. There were no sheets, blankets, food, or toilet paper, just the basic furniture. It was January and very cold. I sat on the empty bed and then decided to walk to the hospital.

My Dream, America

When I got to the hospital, I introduced myself and asked, "May I please have a pillow, a blanket, a roll of toilet paper, a loaf of bread, and some peanut butter?" They seemed amused and I was most grateful. Hungry and ready to eat a sandwich, I used the back of my paintbrush from my art supplies to scoop the peanut butter, as I had no utensils. A church later heard about me and brought some venison. I did not have a pot to cook it in, so the church came back with a plate, a knife, a fork, and a pan. It was so yummy!

I had to get a Texas driver's license, as I only had my International Driver's License and a social security number, so that I could work. I needed a car to attend the Odessa College to study the required psychiatry and pediatrics courses to qualify to write the Texas Nursing Board exams. I could not afford to study both subjects so I only took psychiatry and did my internship at the Big Spring State Hospital a few days a week, worked nights, and, once I got a car, drove to college sixty miles each way from Big Spring to Odessa twice a week. I later got an extra job in a nursing home as a nursing assistant.

I had to get a car. I would walk down to the bank in downtown Big Spring and speak to them about getting a repossessed car. I did not have credit history in the States, so the answer was no. Each free moment

I had in the day, I would go back to the bank. I had no money either. The bank would not take a chance on me. I would pray and pray for a miracle. One day the loan officer I had been talking to casually told me he played racquetball. I battered my way into that conversation, saying that if I beat him at a game of racquetball, he should then let me build my credit by getting a repossessed car. The next day we met at the racquetball courts at the YMCA. I won the game, and got a Pontiac Grand Am, repossessed, four-door, white, with red leather interior. The year was 1978 and it was a miracle!

I had never driven an automatic car. I'd had a standard Ford Escort in South Africa that needed pushing up hills and had to be placed in second gear going down hills to start. Ford had not brought the Escort to the United States yet, so no one believed I'd had such a car. The production of the Ford Escort began in 1981 in the USA. The Datsun in Canada had also been standard. I was so proud of my Pontiac Grand Am. I polished the seats with furniture polish and one would slip from one end to the other, right out of the car door if it was open. What did I know?

My first winter in Big Spring, it snowed heavily. It was breathtaking. Then the "breathtaking" turned to panic! I could not drive in the snow. A little hill near my house looked like a mountain. I was facing the downhill slope and I put the car gear in reverse. I just knew I could not go fast down this hill if my gear was in reverse. I had a lot to learn.

I was excited about attending college in America. My instructor gave my first paper back to me with big red marks all over the page. I did not understand. She stated I needed to get familiar with Webster. I asked her where I could find Webster, and she replied in the bookstore. The first opportunity I had, I went to the bookstore and asked one of the workers, "Is Webster working today?"

"No Webster works here. Anyone heard of a Webster working here? What is it you wanted to ask Webster--maybe I can help you?"

I showed the worker my paper and said my instructor told me to get familiar with Webster. She looked at me with her mouth open with a crazy, funny look, and then said, "Do you mean the dictionary Webster?"

"Maybe?"

I discovered that I'd learned Oxford English (British English) in South Africa, not "Webster" English. I had to study the dictionary. Again, I had a lot to learn.

Helen Munday

I moved to a small house with a friend I had met, so we could share living expenses. I grew a garden with fresh vegetables. This was my main source of food, as I could not afford much after paying for my car, gas, and utilities. Collecting flat, empty aluminum containers from people who had eaten Hungry Man TV dinners, I would cook my vegetables from the garden and make my own frozen dinners. There were no microwaves at that time.

I enjoyed the outdoors, the Texas sunshine, working in the garden, swimming, and playing racquetball. One day I drove to Colorado City, Texas, to the small Lake, lake Colorado City State Park, which is not far from Big Spring. No one was around, and I clambered onto an old wooden dock, and then jumped in the lake. I swam for half the morning. When I got back to Big Spring, I told some friends what a delightful morning I'd had.

"You what!" they exclaimed.

"I swam in Lake Colorado City, it was grand."

"The lake is full of water moccasins, which are black poisonous water snakes," they said, cringing at what they were telling me.

I nodded and said, "I need to ask more questions before doing anything. That is *very* scary."

My Dream, America

I reached into my mailbox and there was a letter from the Department of Immigration. My working visa was up, as I had completed college, and I had to leave the country a couple of weeks from the date of that letter. I still had my exams to write. Someone told me about a Senator John Tower that might help me. I called the office of the senator and told them I still had to write my exams, go back to college, and take pediatrics as required by the nursing board. I prayed for help. I called the nursing board and they said they could not help me. I received a call back from the senator's office, and they wanted me to come and see them. They wrote a letter to Immigration stating I was going back to college after taking my exams, and an extension of my visa was granted. Another miracle had occurred.

I wrote my exams. The first best friend I had made in Big Spring moved to Waco, Texas, to work in the Veterans Hospital as an RN. She called me one day and said, "Come to Waco and see the bluebonnets."

"What are bluebonnets?"

"Come and see. Move to Waco and you can live at my house until you get your feet on the ground. You could do your pediatrics in Dallas at the children's hospital."

"It sounds so great. I am struggling here in Big Spring, as I am babysitting children at night until two or three in the morning, then getting up and going to work and studying for my exams."

Out of curiosity, I went to the library and looked up blue bonnets, and all the wildflowers that grew in the springtime in central Texas. There was no other way to do research except through the library. In June, 1979, I moved to Waco, Texas, no questions asked. When I moved to Waco, my district for Immigration was in San Antonio and I had to reapply to enter the United States as if I had never been in the country. Dallas had been the Immigration district I reported to while I lived in Big Spring. Dallas was two hours from Waco and it took a lot of money, gas, and time to go and study pediatrics at the Parkland Children's Hospital and the Shiners Hospital for Children in Dallas (a requirement of the nursing board). I did some work there a few days a week, worked several jobs in Waco, and helped take care of my friend's little girl.

In December, 1978, I married in Waco, becoming Helen Atkinson, and remained married for fifteen years. There was a bonus to this marriage, a son. He was two years old and I became Mom. I had no other children.

My Dream, America

In December of 1982, I received my Associate's degree in Applied Science and completed my college requirements, internship, and final state and federal board exams in Nursing Home Administration.

My husband was in politics, and when he asked me if I could help run President Carter's campaign in Central Texas, I agreed. This was the beginning of 1980. All my working life I had nursed and never worked in an administration job; again I needed a miracle. It was a lot of fun running the campaign and I met so many wonderful people and learned so much. Soon after I started, they announced that President Carter was going to come to Waco to TSTI (Texas State Technical Institute, now known as Texas State Technical College, TSTC). They asked me to work with the team to get ready for the president's arrival. Cleared by the Secret Service, I went to work. Not being a citizen of the United States, I felt proud and privileged.

The day came when President Carter arrived in Waco; they assigned me to work with the White House press. The press landed first, then Air Force One. After President Carter spoke, I was told to stand in the lineup to shake his hand as he re-boarded Air Force One. Ten invitations were given to me to invite people I knew to attend the ceremony at the airport. This was a truly amazing experience.

It was after President Carter's campaign that I decided to go into Nursing Home Administration. It had given me a confidence I had never had before. In 1993, I received my Bachelor's degree in Business Administration.

The proud day came when I was to become a citizen of the United States. It was December 13, 1983, in San Antonio. I wore a grey suit and my friends gave me a red-white-and-blue corsage. There were about three hundred other people becoming Americans. The ceremony began. Raising my right hand, I felt pain and joy all mixed up deep down inside of me as I became a citizen of the United States. Tears rolled down my face; my heart was pounding with excitement. The pain, joy, and tears were an emotional good-bye to South Africa and an embracement to being a proud and grateful citizen of the United States. All of the people, all different nationalities being sworn in with me, had their own reasons, their own sense of pride and joy, their own stories of struggles and successes.

The United States gave me opportunities I could have never received in South Africa.

My Dream, America

In 1993, I helped get my mother, sister, brother-in-law, and two nieces to the United States. They were on the waiting list to come to the United States for thirteen years. We all live together in Texas. Five years after arriving in Texas, my mother became a citizen and loved living in the United States. She had been a citizen of Holland, South Africa, and the United States. She died in 2006.

In 1994 I divorced and in 2013 I remarried and happily became Helen Munday. A bonus to this marriage is three daughters and six grandchildren. The son I had raised has seven children. My two nieces, married and one niece has three children and one niece has two children, and so I became a lady of many children.

As a free spirit, I reached far beyond the boundaries that life gave to me.

I am proud to be an American. To me America is strength, honor, and gratitude. Gratitude for the opportunities it has given to me, opportunities I could not have reached if I had stayed in South Africa.

I love America, and I am proud to be an American.

www.ingramcontent.com/pod-product-compliance
Lightning Source LLC
Chambersburg PA
CBHW060542080526
44586CB00012B/826